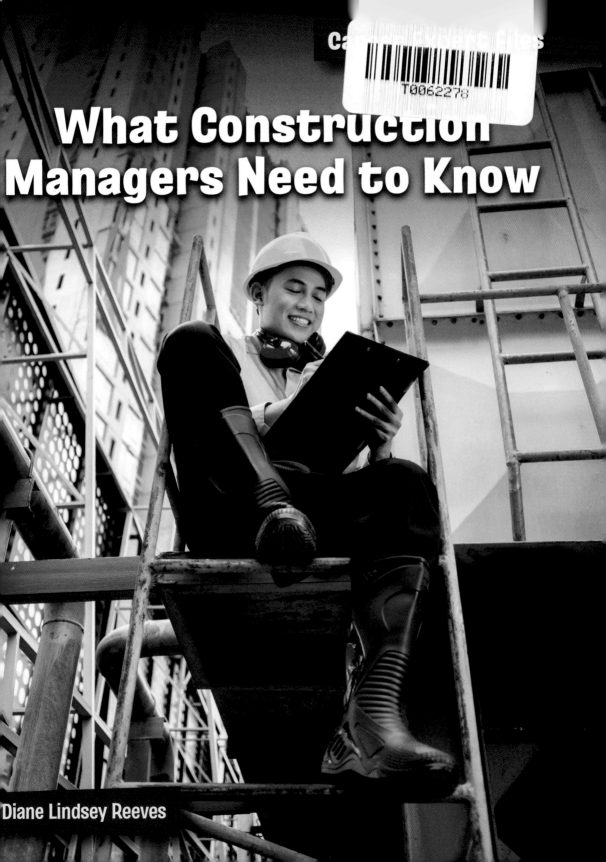

What Construction Managers Need to Know

Diane Lindsey Reeves

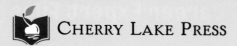
CHERRY LAKE PRESS

Published in the United States of America by Cherry Lake Publishing Group
Ann Arbor, Michigan
www.cherrylakepublishing.com

Reading Adviser: Beth Walker Gambro, MS, Ed., Reading Consultant, Yorkville, IL

Photo Credits: © Kzenon/Shutterstock, cover, 1; © M2020/Shutterstock, 5; © ESB Professional/Shutterstock, 7;
© evgeniykleymenov/Shutterstock, 8; © JU.STOCKER/Shutterstock, 9; © skipper_sr/Shutterstock, 11; © Dmitry
Kalinovsky/Shutterstock, 12; © BearFotos/Shutterstock, 13; © Dragon Images/Shutterstock, 14; © alessandro guerriero/
Shutterstock, 17; © New Africa/Shutterstock, 18; © M2020/Shutterstock, 20; © M2020/Shutterstock, 21; © Volodymyr
Maksymchuk/Shutterstock, 23; © AlyoshinE/Shutterstock, 24; © Elnur/Shutterstock, 25; © BearFotos/Shutterstock, 27;
© RONNACHAIPARK/Shutterstock, 28; © Phovoir/Shutterstock, 29

Cherry Lake Press is an imprint of Cherry Lake Publishing Group.

Library of Congress Cataloging-in-Publication Data

Names: Reeves, Diane Lindsey, 1959- author.
Title: What construction managers need to know / written by Diane Lindsey Reeves.
Description: Ann Arbor, Michigan : Cherry Lake Publishing, [2024] | Series: Career expert files | Includes bibliographical
    references and index. | Audience: Grades 4-6 | Summary: "Construction managers need to have the expert
    knowledge, skills, and tools to keep building bigger and better. The Career Expert Files series covers professionals
    who are experts in their fields. These career experts know things we never thought they'd need to know, but we're
    glad they do"— Provided by publisher.
Identifiers: LCCN 2023035057 | ISBN 9781668939123 (paperback) | ISBN 9781668938089 (hardcover) |
    ISBN 9781668940464 (ebook) | ISBN 9781668941812 (pdf)
Subjects: LCSH: Construction industry—Vocational guidance—Juvenile literature. | Construction workers—
    Juvenile literature.
Classification: LCC TH159 .R443 2024 | DDC 690.023—dc23/eng/20230731
LC record available at https://lccn.loc.gov/2023035057

Cherry Lake Publishing Group would like to acknowledge the work of the Partnership for 21st Century Learning,
a Network of Battelle for Kids. Please visit Battelle for Kids online for more information.

Printed in the United States of America

Diane Lindsey Reeves likes to write books that help students figure out what they want
to be when they grow up. She mostly lives in Washington, D.C., but spends as much time
as she can in North Carolina and South Carolina with her grandkids.

CONTENTS

In the Know

Every career you can imagine has one thing in common. It takes an expert. Career experts need to know more about how to do a specific job than other people do. That's how everyone from plumbers to rocket scientists get their jobs done.

Sometimes it takes years of college study to learn what they need to know. Other times, people learn by working alongside someone who is already a career expert. No matter how they learn, it takes a career expert to do any job well.

Take construction managers, for instance. These professionals know how things get built. Sometimes they also have the skills to build things themselves. They know quality construction work when they see it.

Does the idea of making something out of nothing appeal to you? Do you like working as a team to get big jobs done? Would you like to build a career in construction? Here are some things you need to know.

Construction Managers Are Good at:

- Making busy schedules

- Managing tight (and big!) budgets

- Figuring out the supplies needed for each job

- Supervising other people

- Solving problems and handling conflict

CHAPTER 1

Construction Managers Know... How Things Are Built

Imagine you are standing on an empty street corner. You hold **blueprints** showing plans. They are for a new apartment building. You know how much money there is to build it. You know the time it will take to get it done. Your job? Get it built on time and on budget!

A construction manager knows how to build many things. They know how to build buildings big and small. They know who to hire to do all of the construction jobs. They know where to find the best supplies. They know where to find the best prices. They make plans to keep each job on track.

Construction managers are the project managers of construction.
They make sure each aspect of the job is running smoothly.

Many construction managers work their way
up to managing larger projects.

Many construction managers earn a college degree in construction management. They start with small projects. They work their way up to bigger projects. They spend time at construction sites to get experience. They see how each job is done. They observe skilled workers in action.

A JOB BY ANY OTHER NAME

What do construction managers, project managers, field managers, and builders have in common? They are all different names for the same job. Their job is to make sure that buildings get built right. They're in charge of every step of the process.

CHAPTER 2

Construction Managers Know... Who Builds What

It takes people with many skills to build safe places. These are the places where we live, work, and play. Construction managers know who does what. They know how to get the job done in a **logical** order. They take care of first things first. Then they go on in a way that makes sense. Hint: You don't build the roof first!

Many of the jobs required for construction projects are called **trades**. Tradespeople are experts in specific types of skilled work.

Carpenters are tradespeople often found at a construction site.

Some of the most common trades in construction:

- Carpenters work mostly with wood and nails. They install a building's framework. This includes walls, floors, and doorframes. Some carpenters specialize in building cabinets or furniture.

- HVAC stands for heating, ventilation, and air conditioning. HVAC technicians, also called techs, keep buildings comfortable. They install and repair heating and cooling systems.

- Glaziers cut, install, and remove glass used in windows and doors.

- Electricians wire the systems that power buildings with electricity. They learn this trade in trade school or at a paid apprenticeship. It takes training and experience to become a licensed **journeyman**.

Glaziers know how to handle large pieces of glass safely. They also know how to install it carefully.

Tradespeople, plumbers included, usually train at colleges and institutes. Apprenticeships are a big part of their education.

- Masons use bricks and concrete blocks to build walls and other structures. They may also work with concrete.

- Plumbers work wherever clean water is needed. They install and repair the systems needed for bathrooms. They take care of the systems in kitchens, laundry rooms, and more. Plumbers train as paid apprentices.

- Roofers install, repair, and replace roofs on buildings. They may also install solar panels.

There is an art and a science to these jobs. Some people think anyone can do trade jobs. But that is incorrect. All these trades, and others as well, require skill and talent. Most trade jobs do not require a college education. However, it takes training and experience to become a construction expert.

WHO DOES WHAT WHEN?

Construction managers schedule work in a certain order. Each step builds upon another. Doing things out of order simply won't work.

The following schedule is all mixed up. Grab a piece of paper and number it one through five. Imagine you are building a house. Put each step of the building process in the proper order.

A. Add **insulation** to help keep home temperatures comfortable.

B. Install the wiring and pipes needed for plumbing, electrical, and HVAC systems.

C. Close in the walls with **drywall**.

D. Pour a strong **foundation** for the building to sit on.

E. Frame the house to show where doors, windows, and walls will go.

Answers: 1-D; 2-E; 3-B; 4-A; 5-C.

Construction Managers Know... The Tools of the Trade

Have you ever been to a big tool store like Home Depot or Lowe's? If so, you've probably seen row after row of building tools and supplies. There is a tool for every job and a job for every tool. Different trades require different tools.

Construction workers wear toolbelts to keep basic tools close. Toolbelts are usually made of leather or sturdy canvas. They have pockets and loops for holding different tools. Common tools include hammers, screwdrivers, wrenches, pliers, utility knives, and tape measurers.

Carpenters use hacksaws and circular saws to cut wood. Knowing how to measure accurately is important. Carpenters have a rule: measure twice, cut once. It's a reminder to double-check measurements before making a cut.

Carpenters use circular saws to cut through wood, but these saws are also used

European countries and others use a voltage twice that in the United States. Voltage testers help electricians see if wiring is at the correct voltage.

Working with electricity can be a shocking experience. That's why electricians use voltage testers to run quick safety checks. They do not want to work on live wires or devices. They also use wire strippers, needle-nose pliers,

The first tool glaziers need is safety gloves. These protect their hands from cuts. Glaziers use basic tools like glass cutters. They also use suction cups and putty knives. They have special glazier hammers to carefully tap glass into place. A glazier gun works like a stapler to fasten glass to frames.

HVAC techs use many basic tools. They also use special tools. They use thermometers and gauges. They also use HVAC vacuum pumps. These remove unwanted air and water vapor from AC systems.

A pipe wrench is an important tool for plumbers. They use the wrench to loosen, tighten, and fit pipelines. They use small plumber's torches to **solder** copper pipes together. Drains in toilets and sinks often get clogged. Plumbers use augers and drain snakes to clear them.

FILL YOUR TOOLBOX

Which trade sounds most interesting to you? Ask an adult to help you go online and find images of the tools used to do that job. Draw a picture of a toolbox on a blank sheet of paper. Print out pictures and use them to fill your toolbox with tools.

Harnesses are a must-have for roofers.
Safety is number one!

Installing different roofing requires different tools. Roof tiles, shingles, and steel sheets are all used as roofing.

Roofers work on top of buildings. That's why wearing a safety harness is a must. The harness is clipped to an anchor. If a roofer starts to fall, it catches them in mid air. Roofers use crowbars to remove shingles. They use air knives and snippers to cut shingles. They use nail guns and automatic staplers to attach shingles.

There is a good reason why many tradespeople drive pickup trucks. They need the space to carry all their tools!

CHAPTER 4

Construction Managers Know... How to Build Safely

Construction can be dangerous work. There are four common causes of injuries on construction sites. These include falls and getting struck by objects. These causes also include repetitive motion injuries and electrocution. Cuts, scrapes, bangs, and bruises also come from working with power tools and sharp instruments.

Almost half of all construction injuries happen during the first year on the job. Experience helps keep workers safe. So does common sense and following rules. Taking the time to prepare a work site correctly is important. Using proper safety gear like hard hats, gloves, and knee pads are good safety measures, too.

Hard hats are a common piece of safety gear worn by every member of a construction crew.

EARTH-FRIENDLY BUILDING

Keeping Earth safe is another important challenge. Green building is a process of making smart choices. Smart choices must be made about materials, water, energy, and health.

Green materials come from natural, **renewable**, or recycled sources. For instance, some companies use old shingles to manufacture new ones.

Companies find ways for people to use water more efficiently. This is another way to build green. Some builders include rainwater collection systems in their projects. They also find ways to recycle gray water. Gray water is wastewater from baths, sinks, and washing machines. Even fixing leaky faucets can save up to 20 gallons (75.7 liters) of water a day.

Green builders find many ways to save energy. They may install solar panels as an energy source. They use energy-efficient windows. They use good insulation. These things reduce the energy needed for heating and cooling. Conserving energy also saves people money on utility bills.

About 150,000 construction workers are injured each year on job sites. Staying safe can prevent this!

Yes, accidents happen at construction sites. Training, careful attention, and responsible behavior limit risk. They keep people safe.

CHAPTER 5

Construction Managers Know...How to Find the Job They Want

Construction managers work on projects of all types and sizes. Some own their own businesses. Some are hired by homeowners or builders. Some work for large construction companies.

Construction managers often start with smaller housing projects. This type of job gives them practice. It helps them learn what it takes to build something. It shows them the process from start to finish. Residential projects include single-family homes, apartments, townhouses, and condos.

Many construction managers start with residential home projects. Starting with simpler projects helps them get important experience that will help them with larger projects.

Commercial construction works on buildings used for business. These can be anything from offices to skyscrapers. It also includes stores, shopping malls, hotels, and resorts.

Other types of construction are even more complex. Some examples are institutional projects. These projects include work on buildings for the government. They also include schools and military buildings.

Civil projects include the systems used in transportation. Bridges, roads, railroads, and airports fall into this area.

HELP WANTED

The future of construction is big. There is always a need to build new buildings and repair old ones. But 3 out of 10 construction workers are expected to retire by 2026. The construction industry needs more young people. The industry needs skilled tradespeople to fill demands for new workers.

There are currently about 472,000 construction managers in the United States. They work on many different kinds of projects.

In bigger companies, construction managers may focus on a certain area. They may work on budgets, quality control, or safety. Some handle contracts. These specialists tend to manage more than one project at a time.

Many colleges offer 2- or 4-year degrees in construction management. Working on bigger and more complicated projects requires more education.

All types of construction managers need time to build their careers. They learn from work experience and

Activity

Stop, Think, and Write

Can you imagine a world without construction managers? How do they improve the places where we live, work, and play?

Get a separate sheet of paper. On one side, answer these questions:

- *How do construction managers make the world a better place?*
- *What if you could be in charge of building something amazing in your community?*
- *What's your idea of a dream building project?*

On the other side of the paper:

- *Draw a picture of you showing off in front of the building you built.*

Things to Do If You Want to Be a Construction Manager

Think you might be interested in a career in construction? There are things you can do now and later to find out if this career is a good fit for you.

NOW

- There is always something in need of repair around a house. Ask your parents to let you help fix things.
- Keep an eye on construction projects in your community. Watch how new buildings take shape.
- Volunteer for the youth programs at your local Habitat for Humanity.

LATER

- Find out if your school district offers any high school partnership programs with construction academies.
- Learn one or more construction trades at a technical school and/or apprenticeship program.
- Get lots of experience in construction.
- Check out earning a college degree in construction technology or construction management.

Learn More

Books

Agrawal, Roma. *How Was That Built?* New York, NY: Bloomsbury, 2022.

Cella, Clara. *Underwater Construction Workers.* Minneapolis, MN: Lerner, 2023.

Kerschbaum, John. *Skyscrapers: The Heights of Engineering.* New York, NY: First Second, 2019.

Reeves, Diane Lindsey. *World of Work: Architecture and Construction.* Ann Arbor, MI: Cherry Lake Publishing, 2017.

Rhatigan, Joe. *Get a Job at a Construction Site.* Ann Arbor, MI: Cherry Lake Publishing, 2017.

On the Web

With an adult, learn more online with these suggested searches.

ACE Mentor Program of America

Architecture for Kids

Construct Your Future

Explore the Trades

Glossary

blueprints (BLOO-printz) detailed drawings of an architect's plans for a building

drywall (DRIYE-wawl) a type of board made from plaster, wood pulp, or other material that is used to form the interior walls of buildings

foundation (fown-DAY-shuhn) a solid base on which a building is built, such as a basement, concrete slab, or crawl space

insulation (in-suh-LAY-shuhn) a special material used to stop heat, sound, or electricity from escaping

journeyman (JUHR-nee-muhn) person who has completed an apprenticeship or training program and is fully qualified to do a specific trade without supervision

logical (LAH-jih-kuhl) approaching something in a way that makes sense

renewable (rih-NOO-uh-buhl) something that is not depleted by being used

solder (SAH-duhr) to create a permanent bond between pieces of metal using a fusible metal alloy

trades (TRAYDZ) professions like carpentry and plumbing that are connected with construction projects

Index